Positioning Yourself to Prosper:
How to Create a Life of Abundance Through Purpose

Trasetta Alexander

Positioning Yourself to Prosper

Copyright © 2020 Trasetta Alexander

Unless otherwise noted, scripture quotations are taken from the Holy Bible, KJV.

All rights reserved. No portion of this book may be reproduced, stored in a retrieval system, or transmitted in any form or by any means - electronic, mechanical, photocopy, recording, scanning or other, - except for brief quotations in critical reviews or articles, without the prior written permission of the publisher.

Published in Tallahassee, Florida by Trasetta Alexander Enterprises

www.trasettaalexander.com

ISBN-13: 978-0-578-51442-0

This book is dedicated to those who know they are called for more and are ready to go get it.

CONTENTS

Introduction 1

Chapter One: Entrepreneurship and the Kingdom of God 13

Chapter Two: Called to Abundance 17

Chapter Three: Wisdom: The Principle Thing 33

Chapter Four: Blocks to Prosperity 47

Chapter Five: How to Obtain Abundance 67

Chapter Six: Uncovering Your Purpose 81

Chapter Seven: Increasing Your Capacity 95

Final Thoughts 109

Acknowledgements 111

About the Author 113

About the Author...94

Introduction

Before we dive in, I want to give you a little bit of the backstory to how I came about studying out this topic. At the time of this writing it has been about three years since I began petitioning the Lord for revelation concerning the end time wealth transfer. If you have been in the household of faith for any length of time, you've probably heard pastors or ministers talking about the end time wealth transfer or the transfer of wealth.

There are several scriptures in the Bible which specifically talk about the wealth of the wicked being laid up for the just. So as a result, I got curious about this and wanted to know how it is going to happen.

I started praying regularly, asking the Lord, "How are you going to do this? What will it look like? And when are you going to do it?" Well, about a year ago I was in prayer before worship service and I was just kind of walking the floor praying. I wasn't even praying about the questions I had. I was praying over the service, welcoming His Spirit into the building and magnifying the name of the Lord. All of a sudden, the Lord spoke to me saying, "Do you really want to know about the wealth transfer?" I stopped dead in my tracks.

At first, I was thrown off. I wasn't sure what to say. In my head I'm like, "Um, yeah! I've only been asking you for about two years." But I responded audibly "Yes Lord." What He said to me after that changed my entire mindset about money, success and purpose. He told me "I am positioning my people in places of power and authority in businesses, industries and politics so that they can get deals, negotiations and contracts to bring in the wealth of the wicked into the Kingdom of God".

Wow! Huge right?

While I was blown away by His response, it ended up leaving me with many more questions. And so, I began my journey of searching out the scriptures related to wealth and business. I really started doing a deep dive into the concept of being positioned to prosper, being in a position to gain the wealth of the world.

What He said to me after that changed my entire mindset about money, success and purpose.

At the time I was a year and a half into running my second business start-up, Sister Spotters. My business wasn't growing the way I had anticipated. I was struggling to find clarity around my business positioning. Writing content for my social media, blog posts, website and sales pages was a very laborious process. It just didn't flow the way it did in the beginning. Just a month or so after finally getting the answer from the Lord I had been seeking, I had an encounter with Him.

It was not one of those warm and fuzzy encounters. It was more like Paul's road to Damascus experience. He essentially called me on the carpet about what I was doing in my business. I don't know if you've ever been hemmed up by the Lord but it is NOT pleasant.

He told me the vision He had given me was only part of where He was taking me. I didn't wait on Him to reveal the entire picture. In fact, He gave me an analogy. The most important part of any structure is the foundation.

When you're building the typical home, the foundation can be poured in a single day. However, when you're building something the size of a mall or business complex, the foundation may take a few days or even weeks to be fully poured.

The thing is, you don't start building on the foundation until it's fully laid. What He told me is I started building before the foundation was fully set.

As difficult as it was, I decided right then and there to tear down everything I had built. Um hm...everything "I" had built.

I was right in the middle of launching a program. I had monthly mini mastermind events scheduled. I had just launched a membership program. I had even just finished a total rebrand of my company. But...I let everything go so that I could have ALL God desired me to have.

In full transparency, I did keep the membership program going because I had people who had paid for annual membership and I wanted to honor their purchases.

You might be wondering why I'm sharing this story. You'll see in a moment just how relevant it is to our subject. I want you to understand, it was only when

I was willing to sacrifice all I had worked on over the past 18 months that I tapped into the TRUE purpose for my life.

Over the next 2 months I spent hours in prayer, studying God's Word, and researching prosperity. Letting go opened up my schedule and my heart to receive the message God has me sharing with you now.

In the chapters that follow, I'll be sharing with you why the prosperity message is for right now, how seeking wisdom enables you to call wealth and abundance into your life, some of the most common blocks to prosperity, how to tap into your personal wealth and ways to increase your capacity for more.

We'll cover the reasons we don't have the abundance that God really and truly desires for us to have. For some it is because your focus is off. You are simply focusing on the wrong things.

Your focus is more on the attainment of wealth rather than the one who is the Giver of the wealth. For others, it's going to be that you are not really in integrity with your finances. You're not consistently tithing, or perhaps not at all. Maybe you don't pay our bills on time.

God can't trust you with an abundance of finances, if you're out of integrity with what you already have. Another reason is rebelliousness. When God comes and tries to correct us, we don't want to listen to what He's saying. We want to keep on going our own way, living a life of disobedience rather than in obedience to our loving Father.

Wrong beliefs about money can be another block. I'll touch on five common money myths we believe that are factual, but it's the underlying message holding us back. Sayings like, "money doesn't grow on trees". Yes, we know there aren't any trees out there where you can pluck a few hundred dollar bills off. Lord, I wish there was, but they just don't exist.

The thing is, it's not so much the saying. It's the messaging behind the saying. What is the underlying message? What is the mindset that is attached to that saying? We're going to dig into some of those common money myths and uncover the limiting beliefs behind them.

Then, we're going to move into where the abundance God has for us is. I've already given you a clue. It's in the world. It is already out there in the world waiting for you.

There are thousands of wealthy people in the world who are not believers. They are not followers of Christ. Through negotiating contracts and deals we can bring the wealth of the wicked into the Kingdom of God. Not only that but impact and change life to the glory of God. We can call that into our lives.

The next conversation is, how do I attract into my life the abundance of wealth. How do I call it in? The abundance will come through your purpose. If you haven't already, I'll discuss how to connect with your purpose and why your kingdom purpose is so important.

I believe God created every single individual on purpose and for a purpose. So, we're going to dive deep into the importance of clarifying and connecting with your purpose. We will close out talking about how to increase your capacity.

Once you have figured out what your purpose is, really clarified it and gotten pregnant with this big vision, "how do you get from where you are to where you want to be?"

Often times the reason that grand vision God has for us seems out of reach is because we have maxed out the capacity of our soul. The scripture says in 3 John 1:2, "Beloved, I pray that you may prosper in all things and be in health, just as your soul prospers."

You will never be able to gain prosperity beyond what your soul is able to handle. You have to figure out where those blocks are. Where those areas are in your life, where you are at capacity, so you can then expand, grow and increase your capacity for more to come into your life.

Many times, we're holding on to things. Because we are holding very tightly onto the things we already have, we're not open to receive what God has for us. We have to learn how to release and let go so we can make room for more in our lives.

I'll share some really specific strategies for increasing your capacity. It's all going to begin with personal development. That means you're going to have to work on your mindset. Generally speaking it all comes down to our mindset. It is what you believe holding you back from being able to have more and to grow into a space where you can call more into your experience.

I promise it is going to be good. It is going to be super juicy. I am going to challenge you. I am going to step on your toes a little bit. I'm forewarning you.

If you're ready to position yourself to prosper, keep reading.

Trasetta Alexander

CHAPTER ONE

Entrepreneurship and the Kingdom of God

Throughout the ages, as a society or a world, we have typically been entrepreneurs. In the biblical days and for many, centuries, people worked for themselves. They had some sort of specialty. There were blacksmiths and farmers.

You had lawyers and doctors but there was no institutional business. There were apprentices, workers and servants, but not the big business or industry as we see it in today's society. Working for a company is a relatively new concept which came about as a result of the Industrial Revolution. As factories started popping up, the owners of these companies needed large numbers of people to work for them to produce their products.

The Industrial Revolution began in the early 1900s and ushered in a shift from being an entrepreneurial society to what we see today, a more company or corporation structured economic system. However, God is wanting to move us back into the space of entrepreneurship and position us not only in the marketplace but politics, in high ranking government roles.

The truth is, if anyone in this world ought to be wealthy, it should be God's people

---

I'm not just talking about the local city level. I'm talking about from the city all the way to the nation. God is positioning us in places of power. Also, in corporations where you will see believers as CEOs who can be the innovators and a driving force in their industry, rather than someone who does not hold the values of the Christian faith.

Especially individuals who can disrupt the current system and meet the needs of others with both products and services, as well as spiritually, by being a light for those in the world who are lost. The truth is, if anyone in this world ought to be wealthy, it should be God's people, right?

If you are a child of God, you should be…we should be wealthy. We should be the ones who hold the riches of the world.

I was important for me to lay that foundation because this is what the Lord is speaking to the household of faith. He is putting us in a place of power, authority and influence in the marketplace where were can negotiate deals and contracts that will bring the wealth of the world back into the Kingdom of God where it's intended to be.

Throughout the pages of this book, I will be walking you through what this actually looks like. The very first thing we're going to cover is the fact God wants you to walk in abundance.

CHAPTER TWO

Called to Abundance

But thou shalt remember the LORD thy God: for it is he that giveth thee power to get wealth, that he may establish his covenant which he sware unto thy fathers, as it is this day. ~ Deuteronomy 8:18

There are a great deal of misconceptions about Christians and Christianity. Many people believe Christians should be poor. Especially, when it comes to clergy or the leadership in the church. There are those who think if you are a Christian, you should live a modest life.

However, there are countless scriptures that speak to the contrary. In fact, our foundational scripture for this is John 10:10 where Jesus said, *"The thief cometh not, but for to steal, and to kill, and to destroy: I am come that they might have life, and that they might have it more abundantly."* Jesus is not just talking about health and long life. Jesus came for us to have abundance in every aspect of our life. That includes finances!

For people to think you, as a believer, should live an impoverished life or to live a life of modest means is in direct contradiction to what the Word of God says. Merriam-Webster defines abundance as "a relative degree of plentifulness." However, based on what I've read in the scriptures, God's abundance is a state of overflow.

The God of Overflow

The scripture says in Ephesians 3:20, He's "able to do exceeding abundantly above all we can ask or think." Malachi 3:10 talks about Him pouring out a blessing that you won't have room enough to receive. When Jesus told Peter to go fishing and drop the net, he brought in an abundance of fish.

So much so, he had to call his partners to come help him bring in the haul. All of these scriptures directly contradict the sentiments of those people who say Christians should live a modest or impoverished life. That belief is not in alignment with the scriptures. We'll get into the meat of that a little later.

I want to ask you a question. Are you 100% satisfied with the level of abundance and prosperity you have in your life? Do you have so much abundance in your life that you regularly have to tell God "it's too much, please stop blessing me?" (Okay. So…technically that's two questions)

My guess is, if you are reading this book your answer is a resounding NO.

I have delivered this message countless times in person and I literally have never had anyone raise their hand to say yes. And that's okay because it's not me either. Yet! I'm not at that space either where I have the complete and total overflow I know God desires for us to have as believers.

Another question, if we don't have it - abundance - where is it? We talked about this a little bit already. It's in the marketplace, right? It is already in the world. I also shared how I was seeking the Lord, praying for two years for revelation concerning the end time wealth transfer.

When He finally answered me, what God said was, "I am positioning my people in places of power and authority, in the marketplace, in various industries so they can get deals, negotiations, and contracts to bring the wealth of the wicked back into my Kingdom". As a result of the revelation, I began doing a great deal of study and praying, seeking additional insight, more clarification of how it was going to take place. What it is He really means?

One of the barriers to this concept of us having abundance or walking in abundance is we don't think we deserve it or we it is a sin to have it.

A lot of people hold the wrong belief as Christians, we are supposed to live modestly. That we're not supposed to be in a space of luxury or we're not supposed to have an abundance of wealth. They believe money is the root of all evil, but money is not the root of all evil. It is the *love* of money that is the root of all evil. We'll dive much deeper into that in chapter 4.

For right now, I want to share with you some scriptures to back up this idea or this concept we are called to abundance. That we're called to a place of wealth and prosperity.

It is the love of money that is the root of all evil.

I already shared John 10:10.

> *"The thief cometh not, but for to steal, and to kill, and to destroy: I am come that they might have life, and that they might have it more abundantly." ~ John 10:10*

To dive deeper into it, Jesus literally came to the Earth to restore us back to a state of abundance. We had to be restored to a state of abundance. Due to the fall of Adam, we were under the curse. This caused the enemy to wreak havoc in our lives.

When the scripture talks about abundance, it's not just referring to financial abundance. It is abundance in every single area of your life. If you're experiencing lack in your health. If you're having lack in your social relationships. If you're having lack in love. If you're having lack in peace. If you're having lack in joy. You are not living the abundant life Jesus came for you to have. While my specific focus in this book is on financial abundance, it really applies to every single aspect of your life.

Another familiar passage is Malachi 3:10-12.

"Bring ye all the tithes into the storehouse, that there may be meat in mine house, and prove me now herewith, saith the LORD of hosts, if I will not open you the windows of heaven, and pour you out a blessing, that there shall not be room enough to receive it. And I will rebuke the devourer for your sakes, and he shall not destroy the fruits of your ground; neither shall your vine cast her fruit before the time in the field, saith the LORD of hosts. And all nations shall call you blessed: for ye shall be a delightsome land, saith the LORD of hosts."

Now that sounds like abundance to me! This is a state of overflow. I didn't say it. It comes straight from the Word of God. Those people who say Christians, are supposed to live modest or poor lives, we're not supposed to have financial abundance are directly contradicting what the Word of God says.

I want to prove my case a little bit further. Let's go to the book of Luke. Luke 6:38 says,

> *"Give, and it shall be given unto you; good measure, pressed down, and shaken together, and running over, shall men give into your bosom. For with the same measure that ye mete withal it shall be measured to you again."*

So, as we give, we gain back much more than what we give to others, what we give unto the Kingdom or what we give unto the Lord. Again, the Word of God is talking about running over. It's talking about overflow. It's talking about that abundance.

Let's dig deeper and review Galatians 3:9, which reads, *"So then they which be of faith are blessed with faithful Abraham,"*. We are the seed of Abraham. For those of you who may not know, Abraham was extremely wealthy. He had many servants.

He is another example of the call to abundance that God has for us. We were never intended to lead impoverished lives or go through life in a state of lack and I've got even more evidence for you.

The reason I'm going through all these scriptures is because I really want to lay a solid foundation for all the things that are going to come later. I want you to fully understand you have access to an abundant life. You have a call to a prosperous life. It is scriptural. It is not against what God has for you.

You have a call to a prosperous life.

Allow me to share with you two examples of God's overflow in operation. First, we'll look at Matthew 14:14-21.

> *And Jesus went forth, and saw a great multitude, and was moved with compassion toward them, and he healed their sick. And when it was evening, his*

disciples came to him, saying, This is a desert place, and the time is now past; send the multitude away, that they may go into the villages, and buy themselves victuals. But Jesus said unto them, They need not depart; give ye them to eat. And they say unto him, We have here but five loaves, and two fishes. He said, Bring them hither to me. And he commanded the multitude to sit down on the grass, and took the five loaves, and the two fishes, and looking up to heaven, he blessed, and brake, and gave the loaves to his disciples, and the disciples to the multitude. And they did all eat, and were filled: and they took up of the fragments that remained twelve baskets full. And they that had eaten were about five thousand men, beside women and children.

In this particular situation, Jesus was ministering to a crowd of people. It was 5,000 men plus women and children. When daylight was starting to run out, the disciples came to him and said, look, it's getting late. Let's send these people away. Send them into the city so they can go and get some food. Jesus responded, "No, let us feed them". He took a little boy's lunch, two fish and five loaves of bread, then had the disciples to organize the people and break them into smaller groups.

He took the two fish and five loaves of bread, He blessed it and broke. Jesus gave the pieces to the disciples to distribute to the 5,000 men plus women and children. The scripture goes on to say, after they had done that and all were filled, the disciples took up 12 baskets of fragments.

I don't care how little you have right now, if you give God access to it, He can take it, bless it and break it so it can go way further than in the natural it could ever go. And because He is a God of overflow and abundance you will still have some leftover. This is an illustration of overflow. It is an example of the abundance of God in operation.

The second instance I want to review comes from the book of Luke.

And he entered into one of the ships, which was Simon's, and prayed him that he would thrust out a little from the land. And he sat down, and taught the people out of the ship. Now when he had left speaking, he said unto Simon, Launch out into the deep, and let down your nets for a draught. And Simon answering said unto him, Master, we have toiled all the night, and have taken nothing: nevertheless at thy word I will let down the net. And when they had this done, they inclosed a great multitude of fishes: and their net brake. And they beckoned unto their partners, which were in the other ship, that they should come and help them. And they came, and filled both the ships, so that they began to sink. When Simon Peter saw it, he fell down at Jesus' knees, saying, Depart from me; for I am a sinful man, O Lord. For he was astonished, and all that were with him, at the draught of the fishes which they had taken: And so was also James, and John, the sons of Zebedee, which were partners with Simon. And Jesus said unto Simon, Fear not; from henceforth thou shalt catch men. ~ Luke 5:1-

10

In the passage above, Jesus had been ministering to some people and He was backed up against the seashore. People were starting to crowd around. Jesus saw Peter and his partners washing their nets after a night of unproductive fishing. He asks Peter, let me borrow your boat, because the people were crowding him. Jesus says to Peter, let me get into your boat, and then you push out a little bit so that I can speak to the entire crowd. Peter agreed.

When He was done ministering to the people, Jesus turned to Peter and essentially says, "Thanks for letting me use your boat. Why don't you launch back out into the deep and let down your nets for a catch?" Peter responded, Look, we have spent all night long toiling.

According to Merriam-Webster, that word "toiling" means hard and continuous work; exhausting labor or effort. They had been working in their own strength all night long, using all the skill and all the know how they had for fishing, yet they had caught absolutely nothing. But Peter had sense enough to at least do what the Lord said do.

So, he launches out into the deep, he lets down one of his nets and he brings in a catch so huge, so enormous he had to call to his partners in across the water to have them help him bring in the catch. It was too much for him to handle on his own. It was breaking his nets and sinking his boat. Not only that, but the haul caused Peter's partners' nets to break and their boat began to sink.

This is another case of the overflow of God. Just one more example of the abundance of God. These scriptures I have shared with you, I'm presenting as evidence you are called to a place of abundance.

In the rest of this book, I will share with you the things blocking you from receiving the abundance of God or you fully walking in His abundance. As well as, the ways you can realign or make the shifts necessary to gain access to all God has for you.

Because let's face it, the days are winding down. It's time for us to arise. It's time for the children of God to arise. It's time for us to stand up and take our place in this world. We need to show the world who our God is. The sad truth is, nobody wants to listen to you if you don't have any money. In today's society…

Money = Influence

It is very difficult to have influence or impact without wealth. I want to show you how to position yourself for the abundance of God so that you can increase your impact and your influence for the kingdom of God.

CHAPTER THREE

Wisdom: The Principle Thing

Wisdom is the principal thing; therefore get wisdom: and with all thy getting get understanding. ~ Proverbs 4:7

There is this misconception that as Christians we are supposed to have modest financial status or even take vows of poverty. Simply stated…it is not true. We have already proved that out through the scriptures in Chapter 2.

Now we're shifting our focus to seeking wisdom. If we have been called to abundance, if we have been called to have an abundance of wealth, health and peace, any area of our life not experiencing abundance is in a state of lack.

The question is why? Why don't we have the abundance? Why are we experiencing lack when the Bible clearly says we are called to abundance?

The number one reason we don't have the abundance God desires for us to have is because our focus is off. We're simply not focusing on the right things. When it comes to wealth, if we don't have the money we need in order to do what we are called to do or navigate this life, what happens is we end up being so focused on pursuing the wealth that it alludes us. We end up compromising and doing things that we would not normally do because we are chasing after wealth. We're trying to "make" it happen. If that is the case, our focus is off.

When you seek wisdom, wealth comes with it

We should be seeking *wisdom* rather than wealth. The thing is, when you seek wisdom wealth comes with it. Wealth is actually attached to wisdom. I want to go over a couple of verses in the book of Chronicles. Specifically, 2 Chronicles 1:11 - 12.

It's important for me to prove out to you scripturally, this concept of wealth being tied to wisdom. Let me give you the backstory before we get into the verses. King David has died and Solomon, his son, has taken over as king. He has been anointed as king in David's place. He's probably in his early 20s, so he's a really young king when he begins to reign. After stepping into kingship, Solomon goes up and begins to worship the Lord. This was no ordinary worship. This was an extravagant worship before the Lord.

Quick side note: when you begin to worship God extravagantly, He stands up and takes notice. You can guarantee He's going to come and ask, "What is it that you want from me?" When you worship God in that fashion, it's almost as if God has no choice but to come and ask what your petition is. Because extravagant worship only comes from a true heart of worship.

> *"And Solomon went up thither to the brasen altar before the Lord, which was at the tabernacle of the congregation, and offered a thousand burnt offerings upon it. In that night did God appear unto Solomon, and said unto him, Ask what I shall give thee. And Solomon said unto God, Thou hast shewed great mercy unto David my father, and hast made me to reign in his stead. Now, O Lord God, let thy promise unto David my father be established: for thou hast made me king over a people like the dust of the earth in multitude. Give me now wisdom and knowledge, that I may go out and come in before*

this people: for who can judge this thy people, that is so great?" ~ II Chronicles 1:6 – 10

Extravagant worship only comes from a true heart of worship.

What Solomon does is offer up 1,000 burnt offerings unto the Lord as worship. One thousand!! This is an extravagant worship unto the Lord. Afterwards, God appears to him and says, "Ask what you want and I will give it to you." Wow! Because Solomon worshiped God so extravagantly, God essentially gives Solomon a blank check. I'll give you anything you want. Just ask Me.

What most of us would have asked for is riches or other material possessions. Not Solomon! He didn't ask for the riches of the world. He didn't ask for his kingdom to be expanded. He didn't ask for fame. He didn't ask for any of the things that you might think he would ask for.

What did Solomon request from God? He asked for...wisdom. Solomon is known for being the wisest king to have ever reigned in history. It's because he specifically asked God for wisdom.

In verse 10, he says "Give me now wisdom and knowledge that I may go out and come in before this people for who can judge this thy people that is so great". He asked for wisdom in order to do right by the people God put him in charge of. Again, he didn't ask for riches, power or fame. He asked God for wisdom after he worshiped him in this extravagant way. How does God respond?

> *"And God said to Solomon, Because this was in thine heart, and thou hast not asked riches, wealth, or honour, nor the life of thine enemies, neither yet*

hast asked long life; but hast asked wisdom and knowledge for thyself, that thou mayest judge my people, over whom I have made thee king: Wisdom and knowledge is granted unto thee; and I will give thee riches, and wealth, and honour, such as none of the kings have had that have been before thee, neither shall there any after thee have the like."

~ 2 Chronicles 1:11-12

God tells him, I'm going to give you wisdom and knowledge just like you asked for but He doesn't stop there. He goes on to say, "and I will give thee riches and wealth and honor such as none of the kings have had that have been before thee. Neither shall there any after thee have the like."

As a result of Solomon's extravagant worship God gives him the blank check and says, "Ask what you want". Solomon asked for wisdom, but God goes "exceeding, abundantly above" that (as is His nature) and gives him wealth, honor and riches. This is why I'm saying we need to seek wisdom. The book of Proverbs talks about wisdom giving us knowledge of witty inventions. Also, in the book of Deuteronomy it says God has given us the power to get wealth.

I wisdom dwell with prudence, and find out knowledge of witty inventions. ~ Proverbs 8:12

But thou shalt remember the Lord thy God: for it is he that giveth thee power to get wealth, that he may establish his covenant which he sware unto thy fathers, as it is this day.

~ Deuteronomy 8:12

If we're not supposed to have wealth, why would God give us the power to get it? It's through the wisdom that we obtain the financial wealth, the riches we truly desire. Asking for the heart of God, the wisdom of God brings forth the hand of God also. Wisdom actually attracts wealth. Let's take a look at I Kings.

I want you to see this in the Word because as a faith-based business coach everything I teach my clients is in alignment with the Word of God. I want to make sure, first and foremost, we're serving Him. There are a lot of coaches out there. There are a lot of experts out there. There are a lot of gurus out there, but what they teach isn't necessarily in alignment with our faith and with our beliefs as Christians.

Matter of fact, often times what they teach is in direct contradiction of the Word of God. I want to make sure whenever I'm sharing strategies, techniques, and business practices, they are in alignment with our beliefs as Christians. 1 Kings 10:23-25 says,

> "King Solomon exceeded all the kings of the earth for riches and wisdom and all the Earth sought to

Solomon to hear his wisdom, which God had put in his heart and they brought every man his present vessels of silver and vessels of gold and garments and armor and spices, horses and mules at a rate year by year".

Just as with Solomon, when you have wisdom, wealth is automatically attracted to you. When you have wisdom, people will seek you out and willingly pay you for your wisdom. That's what an expert or a consultant does. Even myself as a coach, have knowledge others desire to have.

People pay me for that information and knowledge so they don't have to do all the research themselves or go through the process of trying to figure it out on their own. They can shortcut the system by going directly to someone who's already done the work. Someone who's done the research, and is able to filter out the unnecessary information to bring forth that which is most valuable.

For example, let's say there's a book on a particular subject and I've already read the book. I can extrapolate all the content out of it that is actionable and condense it into little bite size pieces. Now someone else could come to me, get those bite sized pieces and they don't necessarily have to go read the whole book. They can save time by hiring me to share with them the knowledge and wisdom I've gained. So, you see, wisdom attracts wealth.

When you really and truly desire wealth, the focus needs to shift from desiring the wealth to focusing on desiring the wisdom. It is the wisdom which will attract the wealth to you. Work on being who God called you to be. By doing so the blessing will come and overtake you.

God always provides for what He has purposed.

I believe God has a specific purpose for each of us. That purpose is the reason we were born. Whatever our purpose is, He has attached our prosperity to it. So, by tapping into why you're here or your purpose then executing it brings the prosperity to you because you are in alignment with your purpose.

God always provides for what He has purposed.

You're stepping into the space or the environment, I like to say your purpose environment, for which you were created to thrive, grow and flourish. It is only when you step into your purpose and you do the thing that God called you to do, the blessing comes and overtakes you. You won't have to chase after prosperity, like others do.

Too many people are chasing after prosperity and it's alluding them. That's why some people never seem to get enough. Greed sets in because they're chasing after the wealth or chasing after the riches or they are chasing after the fame. It never seems to be enough.

It will never be enough. It won't create the joy you think it will. When I get to this income amount, then I'll be happy. You'll get there and it's like, okay, it's not enough. So, you adjust. Well, when I get to this amount, then I will be happy. Or when I get to this amount, I will be happy. Sad to say, the end is never in sight.

If you're looking for wealth to fulfill you...IT WILL NEVER BE ENOUGH!

If you are chasing after prosperity, you will never be satisfied or fulfilled. On the contrary when you chase after wisdom and do the thing that God created you to do, you will draw in the prosperity you truly desire. Your focus has to be on doing what you were created to do so the prosperity will find you.

In the next chapter, we're going to get into some of the specific reasons or blocks to the flow of prosperity in your life. I encourage you to focus on seeking wisdom. Get into the space of praying and seeking wisdom from God. Wisdom isn't just about gaining prosperity. It can also help us know when we're making a bad deal, when we're making a bad business decision, or not even necessarily in business decision, but a decision for our lives. God will lead us and guide us by His Spirit, when we seek that wisdom.

When we seek knowledge from Him. Then we can get His direction and know we're taking the right path. We'll know we're on the right course for where it is that He would desire to go.

CHAPTER FOUR

Blocks to Prosperity

Now we're getting into the meat of this topic. This chapter will cover the three major blocks to your prosperity. I'm going to be honest with you. I am probably going to step on your toes just a little bit. I know it may be uncomfortable, but this is real good stuff. If you can get rid of these blocks, you'll make a clear pathway for prosperity to come into your life. If a particular block hits you, just say ouch and keep on reading. You can't fix what you don't know is broken.

Financial Integrity

The first block to your prosperity is not operating in integrity with your finances.

What do I mean by that?

One of the things that we're called to do as believers is to give 10% of all of our income to the Lord. This is the tithe. In Malachi is says 10% belongs to the Lord; the tithe is not ours. It does not belong to us. It belongs to God. When we don't tithe regularly, or don't tithe that all, we are out of integrity with our finances. One of the things the scripture declares is when we tithe it rebukes the devour.

> *Bring ye all the tithes into the storehouse, that there may be meat in mine house, and prove me now*

herewith, saith the Lord of hosts, if I will not open you the windows of heaven, and pour you out a blessing, that there shall not be room enough to receive it. And I will rebuke the devourer for your sakes, and he shall not destroy the fruits of your ground; neither shall your vine cast her fruit before the time in the field, saith the Lord of hosts. And all nations shall call you blessed: for ye shall be a delightsome land, saith the Lord of hosts. ~ Malachi 3:10-12

Tithing keeps the enemy from stealing our riches. It keeps him from stealing our wealth, the monies, the abundance that we have. If you're not tithing at all or regularly, then you are out of integrity with your finances and that opens the door for Satan to devour your finances.

Tithing keeps the enemy from stealing our riches.

The way I like to look at it is, the 10% that belongs to God, is our franchise fee. It is the way we gain access to all the resources of heaven. If you think about a franchise here in the natural, what happens is a person wants to open up a franchise of an overarching institution and they pay a franchise fee to do so. Rather than them going off and starting, let's say like for example, a McDonald's or another fast food restaurant on their own and having to come up with a menu, all the systems and processes they're going to need, all the training manuals, they can go to the McDonald's Corporation and pay a fee to join the franchise. The franchise fee then gives them access to all of the resources that McDonald's has.

It's the same way with our tithe. Our tithe is like our franchise fee to gain access to all the resources of heaven, to gain access to all that God has. When we don't pay our fee or we don't give of our tithe, we block access.

For instance, if you have a membership and you don't pay your membership fee then your access is restricted. You no longer have access until you come up-to-date with your membership fees. It's the same way with our tithe. When we're withholding our tithe, our access to the resources of heaven are restricted. We aren't able to grab hold of all that God has for us.

This is why it's important for you to tithe regularly. Usually pastors will share the scripture in Malachi when it's time for you to give your offering or to give your tithe. The scripture talks about "bring ye all the tithes and offerings into My storehouse that there may be meat in My house".

Going further into that passage, it states "will a man rob God" and He says, "yet you have robbed me of tithes and offerings." This is what the scripture is talking about. The tithe belongs to God already. God gives us the opportunity to partner with Him, to give to Him. While it belongs to Him, He entrusts it with us and then we are responsible for giving back to Him what is His, unlike our government, who takes their cut before we get what is ours.

We are essentially misappropriating funds when we use the 10% that belongs to God. When you are out of integrity with your finances in this way, when you're not tithing, you are blocking the flow of prosperity to your life. I know this is kind of tough to hear, but the whole purpose of me sharing this with you is so that you can get in alignment with the abundance of God. One of the ways you do that is to be consistent in the giving of your tithe.

Many people feel like, "I can't afford to give that 10%. I need all of it because I already don't have enough or I barely have enough to get by off of what I bring in".

We're so focused on the "giving up" of that 10%, we don't realize we gain so much more when we give to God and partner with Him. We gain access to all He has, every resource of heaven. We invite Him to open doors of opportunity for us and for Him to make a way for us by the giving of our tithe.

In February 2012, I decided to take a leap of faith and quit my job so that I could go back to school. I wanted to really figure out what it was God was calling me do because I knew where I was and what I was doing, wasn't it.

I hit a wall. I felt like there has to be more. I knew, with all that was in me, there was more. I also knew I wasn't going to find it where I was. When I quit, I didn't have another job to go to. I just believed it was what God was calling me to do: to trust Him in this new way. I knew it was going to be challenging because I had never done this before.

Every time I had ever left any job, I had another one to go to. I needed something tangible to hold onto when things got difficult. I knew at some point my faith would be tested. I knew I might feel like I was losing hope and I wanted a physical reminder of what I was believing God for. Even if I couldn't necessarily see what God was doing, I would know He was still at work.

I knew, with all that was in me, there was more.

I decided to plant some gladiola bulbs right in front of our apartment. We had a little garden area right alongside the walkway, leading up to the apartment. One thing about a seed: when you plant something in the ground, the first thing it does is it goes down. The roots start to grow down in the dirt and it takes a little while before you see evidence of the growth above the ground. However, as soon as you put it in the ground, the seed starts to germinate and grow and eventually it will start breaking through the ground and sprouting.

Every day after I planted the gladiola bulbs, I would go outside and water them. As I watered them, I would pray. I would pray over my situation. I would pray over the circumstance and continue to believe God would open a door of opportunity for me. There were 12 bulbs I planted in the ground. A few weeks later, they started popping up. I started seeing little sprouts coming up out of the ground and all of them came up, except for one.

There was one of the bulbs which just did not seem to want to sprout. The other ones were growing and flourishing and this other one just wasn't coming up. I became so obsessed with the one that was not coming up to the point where one day I thought to myself, "You know what? Maybe I put it in upside down. Maybe I did something wrong. Let me dig it up so that I can check on it to see what's wrong with it".

I had my little gardening shovel in my hand and just before I got ready to stick it in the ground to dig up the bulb, I heard the voice of the Lord tell me to leave it alone. He said, "Don't touch it. It will come up when it's time." Why am I telling you this story?

A lot of times, like I was with that one bulb, we are so focused on what we don't have we miss out on what we do possess. That 10%, the tithe, we give to God is so small but it can do so much when we give it to Him and allow Him to have access into our financial life. He can then bless us financially. He can open doors for us. With the invitation into our finances through our tithe we partner with Him.

When you are not consistently giving your tithe, the10% which belongs to the Lord you are out of integrity with your finances. Not paying your bills on time consistently or avoiding creditors, is another way you can be out of integrity with your finances.

One thing about God, He is a God of order. He is not going to bless something out of alignment with truth, honesty and integrity. We have to do our part to make sure we stay in integrity with our finances by paying our bills on time to the best of our ability and the giving of our tithe.

Of course, things come up from time to time, but I'm talking about instances where you intentionally pay bills late to do something you *want* to do or you avoid creditors because you don't have the money. Be diligent about paying your bills on time or corresponding with your creditors if something comes up and you're not able to be timely in your obligation.

A Rebellious Heart

The second block to your prosperity is you are a rebel Christian. Maybe you have a rebellious heart. You don't want to follow the Word of God or you refuse correction. When you're in that space of disobedience, you refuse to follow the Word of God or you refuse to be corrected by the Word of God, then you are essentially in a state of rebellion.

Again, God desires for us to be obedient to His Word. Not like dogs where we have to be subservient. This obedience is an act of worship. It's an act of trust because He knows what's best for us. It is through being obedient to His word and doing what His word says that we open the door for the blessing to come in.

Money Mindset

The third block to your prosperity is your money mindset. There are some money myths you believe blocking you from gaining the prosperity God really has for you. In 3 John 1:2, it says,

> *"Beloved, I wish above all things that thou mayest prosper and be in health, even as thy soul prospereth".*

Our soul acts as the thermostat for the amount of prosperity that we can have. If we don't grow and develop our soul man, (that is your mind, your will, and your emotions), we will self-sabotage. If we have a blessing come into our lives and we have not prospered our soul, what happens is we subconsciously sabotage ourselves and essentially forfeit the blessing.

As I am writing this book, it's tax season and Monday our tax returns are due. If you get a tax refund, large or small, and it is spent before you ever receive it, perhaps you have not prospered in your soul. Or suppose you get a large sum of money, such as a bonus at work, but some emergency comes up which eats up the majority, if not all of the money. This is a sign you may not have developed your soul.

There are a few money myths we believe or rather the mindset behind the sayings which trip us up. We say these things over and over, solidifying the belief in our subconscious mind. While the saying itself is factual, the concept behind it or the underlying message is not. That is what we're holding in our heart, the mindset.

There are no limits to the amount of wealth available in the world.

Money Myth # 1 - Money doesn't grow on trees.

The most popular one is "money doesn't grow on trees". Yes, that is correct. We all know this to be true. There is no money tree out in my yard where I can just go pluck off some hundred dollar bills, or even $1 bills, for that matter. While the saying is true, the mindset behind it or the spirit behind it is there's a limited amount of money available in the world. That is simply not true.

There are no limits to the amount of wealth available in the world. There is an unlimited supply. However, there used to be a limited amount of currency because all US dollars had to be backed by gold. This is called the gold standard. In 1973, the US officially ended its adherence to the gold standard. It is this outdated standard where the mindset originated.

Because money is no longer backed by gold, there is no limit to the amount of money available.

By saying "money doesn't grow on trees", you're actually insinuating there's not enough to go around. You are affirming money is not a renewable resource. You're putting a cap on the amount of finances or the amount of money you can call into your life.

Money Myth #2 – Money is evil.

Another money myth is, money is evil. I talk about this one a lot. It is one you have probably heard often. But that isn't what the scripture says.

> *"For the love of money is the root of all evil: which while some coveted after, they have erred from the faith, and pierced themselves through with many sorrows." ~ 1 Timothy 6:10*

It says that the *LOVE* of money is the root of all evil. It's not money itself. Money is actually an inanimate object. It can't be either good or evil. It has no personality because it is not a living being. What happens is it takes on the personality of the person who uses it. Someone who is good and uses money for good, good things happen.

For example, they might donate money to charity or buy a meal for someone who is hungry. On the contrary, someone who is evil or has wicked motives and takes their money to use it for evil or wicked things, like buying drugs or to bribe someone in a position of power it produces bad things.

Again, money in and of itself doesn't have a personality, but the people who use the money are the ones who are expressing the personality of good or evil.

Money Myth #3 – Rich people are selfish.

The next money myth is, rich people are selfish. While many believe this, it is untrue. I want to share with you a few statistics. The first is the top 1% of people in the U.S. regarding wealth, provide one-third or 33% of all charitable donations. Additionally, the top 1.4% account for 86% of charitable donations at the time of death.

In other words, they're leaving some sort of endowment or trust to one or more charitable organizations. The remaining 14% comes from the other 98.6% of the population. As you can see, this idea that rich people are selfish, simply isn't true. Don't get me wrong. I am not naive enough to believe all rich or wealthy people are generous. There will always be those who are outliers. I'm simply pointing out this is not the majority.

When you believe people who are rich are selfish, why would you ever want to be rich? You would subconsciously repel wealth because you don't want to become a selfish person. A lot of people sabotage themselves or hold themselves back from having the abundance, having the prosperity, they truly desire because they don't want to become selfish.

You're not going to become selfish just because you become wealthy.

You're not going to become selfish just because you become wealthy. You're just going to do more of what you already do. Money brings out what's already in you. So, if you are already a selfish person, then it's just going to magnify your selfishness. If you are a giving person, it's going to magnify your generosity. This is why it is so important to prosper your soul.

Let's look at this in a case study.

You've likely heard a story or two about someone who won millions of dollars in the lottery and in just a few years they were broke again. For example, William Post won $16.2 million in the Pennsylvania lottery but within a year was $1 million in debt. We can also look at single mother, Sharon Tirabassi, who one $10 million and spent it all on a lavish lifestyle and a less than 10 years later was back to her prior lifestyle of riding the bus living in a rented home.

This happened because they had not prospered their soul. Their soul could not handle the infusion of money all at once, so they ended up right back where they were before they even won the lottery and for some even worse off.

Money Myth #4 – Christians are supposed to be poor.

The last myth I'm going to share is, Christians are supposed to be moderate or poor. I've already covered this a great deal, so I'm not going to belabor the point. I've already proven it out through the scriptures in Chapter 1. God's desire is for us to be prosperous and to have abundance. We're not called to be moderate or poor. We are called to live a life of abundance. If we can get rid of these blocks to our prosperity, we will be better positioned to help the poor, to help the needy, to do some of the amazing things we really desire to do, to help others and ourselves.

Those are the most common blocks to your prosperity. Now that we have identified the blocks, we're going to delve into how to get this prosperity or abundance God is calling us to. If you're ready to grab hold of His abundance for your life, read on.

CHAPTER FIVE

How to Obtain Abundance

"A good man leaveth an inheritance to his children's children: and the wealth of the sinner is laid up for the just." ~ Proverbs 13:22

In the book of Proverbs, the scripture talks about how the wealth of the wicked is laid up for the just. Then in Deuteronomy 8:18, it also talks about how God has given us the power to get wealth. The abundance, *your abundance,* is already out there in the world waiting for you. The question we need to ask ourselves is "how can we align ourselves to bring in that abundance, bring in the wealth, into our lives and the Kingdom of God to enable us to advance God's agenda. How would we get it?

The abundance, your abundance, is already out there in the world waiting for you.

We have been in the information age for a while, but we're experiencing a shift. Now we are shifting into an innovation age. While doing some research I read, by 2030 the internet benefits will result in $190 trillion in economic gain worldwide. $190 trillion! Not a million. Not even a billion, but $190 trillion! That is a whole lot of money to be gained worldwide.

I don't know about you, but I would like to take part in some of that economic gain. We already debunked the myth in Chapter 4 that there is a limited amount of money available. In fact, there is plenty of money to go around. So, there is no scarcity. There is no limitation to the amount of money in the world. Someone else being rich, someone else being wealthy does not limit the amount of wealth you can have in your own life. There's more than enough money out there for everyone.

I opened up this chapter by talking about how we're moving into an age of innovation. While we've experienced great innovations, they typically have been by inspiration. Meaning, innovators have been inspired by things around us. Maybe they are products or different things that we've wanted to improve upon. Or, we've seen something which bugs us and we want to improve upon that.

People have been innovating by inspiration because of something outward they've seen and inspired them to say, "Oh, you know what? I wonder if I could do X". Maybe you get a completely different idea because of something else you came in contact with.

However, the innovation age we're moving into is one of innovation by revelation rather than innovation by inspiration. This is not because of something you've seen in the world. It's going to come by the Spirit. It's going to come by revelation. It's going to come by divine download or divine insight as opposed to being inspired by something outwardly.

One thing about innovation is it disrupts the norm. It disrupts the status quo. According to the scriptures, we are the standard not the world. It should not be the other way around. We are the ones who are to set the standard. As God's innovators, we are here to disrupt the norm. We are here to disrupt the status quo. We are *supposed* to be disruptors. We're supposed to be wave makers. We're supposed to be feather rufflers. But instead, what has happened is we have become tolerant and complacent.

> *We are here to disrupt the status quo.*

There has not been much power in the church as of late because we have gotten to the place where we look so much like the world it's hard to see a difference. But the time has come for us to arise as a body of believers, as followers of Christ. It is time for us to arise and raise THE standard. Raise God's standard again and disrupt what is going on in the church first. Stop being so tolerant and politically correct or passive in what we're doing in the body of Christ.

It's evidenced by a myriad of things happening in the church. Scandals, adultery and embezzlement run rampant. The church unfortunately looks a lot like the world of business and politics. Some of the ministries we watch on television look like you're at some sort of pop culture music concert. The backdrop is black and the lights are down low. They've got dry ice smoke and pulsating lights. Jesus dwells in the light.

Why do we have the lights down low in church? We are supposed to be light. We're supposed to be salt in the earth. However, we're so busy trying to entertain people and create an experience, that we're actually losing the true character and standard of God. If we would step back into our kingdom position and raise the standard again we will be the disruptors and influencers we are called to be.

God never called us to be like the world. The scripture 1 Peter 2:9 talks about us being a peculiar people and a royal priesthood. We are supposed to be different. We're supposed to stand out. We're supposed to be polarizing.

Jesus was the same way. The scribes and the Pharisees did not like Jesus saying and doing a lot of things He did because He was shaking up their political and economic system. He was messing with their belief system. We have to step into this revelatory innovation age so we can disrupt the current status quo.

The way to do that is through our purpose, our calling. It is through the very thing God created us to do. How we're going to get the prosperity Jesus died for us to have is through our purpose. In fact, our prosperity is directly tied to our purpose.

The innovative revelations will come to the people of God who are in relationship with Him. I'm not talking about people who just go to church. I'm talking about people who spend time in His Word, who spend time in prayer, who spend time worshiping Him and wait to hear from Him. Those are the people who God will speak to. He's going to be downloading those divine revelations and insights, which will yield witty inventions and witty ideas.

In the book of Proverbs, there's a verse where it talks about how wisdom will give us knowledge of witty inventions.

"I wisdom dwell with prudence, and find out knowledge of witty inventions." ~ Proverbs 8:12

That is innovation! If you want the creative ideas to carry out your purpose in the earth and reap the harvest of the prosperity God is calling you to, it will be through your purpose.

The catch is you have to be in relationship with Christ. You see, pursuing your purpose is an act of worship. It is being obedient to God and the scripture says obedience is better than sacrifice. Whatever God is calling you to do, whatever instruction He's given you, you're only going to get the directive by being in conversation with Him.

As you're in fellowship with Him, He will give you direction. He will give you instruction. He will give you knowledge. He will give you ideas and He will give you the ways to carry them out.

A lot of times it's not going to look like how the world would do it. He will at times tell you to do something completely different than the way the world has historically done something similar. As you carry it out, as you do the thing He has instructed you to do, it is worship unto God. When you withhold, when you delay, when you are not walking in your calling or purpose, you are in disobedience.

There are people who need your gifts, skills, talents, and abilities.

As I mentioned earlier, disobedience is one of the blocks to obtaining the prosperity and abundance God has for you. In order to have it and have it in full flow you must be in total alignment with the thing God created you to do. Anything else is disobedience.

Not only is your prosperity tied to your purpose but there are people who are waiting for you to show up for them. There are people who need your gifts, skills, talents, and abilities. If you don't ever show up, they might not ever get the help they need. They may not ever get the answers they need to their situations and circumstances so they can go forth in life.

It is time for us to stop sleeping and stalling on our calling and start pursuing the thing God created us to do. It is through us actually pursuing our purpose we will gain the prosperity and abundance He has called us to.

One of the illustrations I like to use is a fish. A fish was created to swim. His natural environment is water. He has gills that enable it to breath. As he's in the water, he draws in the water and filters out the air from the water, which gives him his breath. He is able to easily navigate through the water because of his body's design.

On the contrary, if you take a fish and put it on the floor, it's going to flop around. It's going to be gasping for air. It will not be able to swim. It's not going to be able to operate in its purpose because it is outside of the environment that enables it to be most effective and most efficient. The fish is outside of its purpose environment.

It is the same way with us. When we are not in alignment with the thing God called us to do, we are like a fish out of water. We will go through life struggling, flopping around, floundering our way through because we can't operate effectively outside of our purpose environment.

> *When we are not in alignment with the thing God called us to do, we are like a fish out of water.*

It is a struggle. It is a strain. In trying to do it we are frustrated and unfulfilled. But if you align yourself with the thing God created you to do and step into your purpose environment, then you'll be able to flow. You'll be able to soar. You'll be able to fly. You will experience fulfillment. It will come with ease because you are in the environment you were created for, instead of flopping around in a foreign environment suffocating to death.

Unfortunately, a large portion of the world's population is doing this. People are going to a job day in and day out, spending 40 plus hours a week working in a position they don't even like.

According to an article on Huffington Post, there are actually 900 million people across 142 countries who don't like the work they do (figures based on study by Gallop). Here in the U.S., 70% of workers hate their job, but yet they get up day in and day out to go to this place they don't even like.

They spend the majority of their life doing something they dislike, struggling, suffering and unfulfilled. But yet they have this burning desire on the inside of them for more. They know they are called to more. They know they're called to greatness. They know they're called to purpose. Butt because of fear, a lack of confidence or self-esteem or feeling like they don't have the necessary skills and resources, they refuse to pursue it. They don't go after it and end up going through life struggling, never stepping into their true purpose.

The reason I'm sharing this with you is because I want you to actually take the first step and move forward into the thing God called you to. Step into what God specifically created you to do, so you can walk in the abundance He has for you and be fulfilled. The only way you're going to find your fulfillment in this life is if you do what God called you to do. This is the only way.

But what if you don't know what your purpose is? I'll walk you through the steps to take to help you connect with your calling in the next chapter.

CHAPTER SIX

Uncovering Your Purpose

"Call unto me, and I will answer thee, and shew thee great and mighty things, which thou knowest not." ~ *Jeremiah 33:3*

In this chapter I will answer a question I get quite a bit, which is how do I find my purpose? How do I actually go about through the process of uncovering what God created me to do? How do I know what it is God is calling me to do?

Before I actually answer that question, I want to remind you every single one of us was created on purpose and for a purpose. And whatever our purpose is, our prosperity is directly connected to it. Because of this it is critical for you to identify your purpose so you can begin to operate in it.

Many people struggle day to day going to their job. I've been there personally. There was a time when I literally would sit in the parking lot and pray before I would go into my office building because I was so miserable on my job. I was extremely unhappy and I needed the Father's help to get through every single day.

The reason it was such a struggle is because I was operating outside of my purpose environment. I was, for all intensive purposes, a fish out of water.

Just like I shared in the previous chapter, if you take a fish and put him on dry ground, he will flop around gasping for air and not be able to do what he was designed to do.

We're the same way. Our purpose is the same way for us. If we are not in alignment with our purpose, if we're not operating in our purpose environment, we're going to struggle. We're going to be flopping around on the ground gasping for air because we're being suffocated by where we are. Not literally, but figuratively. I want to help you identify what your purpose is so if you're not operating in it you can shift into it. When you do you will not just survive but thrive.

Operating in your purpose enables you to thrive, prosper and grow. I have 5 questions you need to ask yourself in order to uncover your purpose then I'll share a few tips on how to start making the shift into it. Before we dive into the questions, grab a few sheets of blank paper or your journal to answer them as we go along.

Operating in your purpose enables you to thrive, prosper and grow.

Question 1: What am I really good at?

The very first question you need to ask yourself is what are my skills? What are my strengths? What are the things that I'm really good at? What are the things I'm good at naturally? What are the things people ask me to do regularly that just come easy to me, but are more challenging for them to do?

Don't hold back here. You don't have to be the best right now, just willing to become the best. The first step is to identify what is it that you are really good at.

Question 2: What am I deeply passionate about?

The second question you need to ask yourself is, what am I really passionate about? A lot of times when we ask this question or we think about what we're passionate about, we gravitate to the positive. I really enjoy this or I really love doing that. Well, it could be something negative. It could be something which bothers you.

Perhaps during the winter time something you're really bothered by is seeing kids who don't have the proper winter attire. Maybe you pass by a neighborhood bus stop every day and see kids standing out in the cold with just a hoodie or light weight jacket and not a proper coat and it really upsets you or makes you angry.

It could be something that just really bothers you as opposed to it being something that you really enjoy. So don't just think in the positive. Also think about what gets under your skin.

Question 3: What are my values?

The third question I want you to ask yourself is what are my values? What is the belief system I hold? What is a non-negotiable for me?

It could be your faith. It could be integrity. Perhaps you really value relationships. Whatever it is that is important to you, list those out.

I've included a list of common personal values to help you get started. Limit your list to no more than 3 - 5 values.

Common Values

Authenticity	Achievement	Adventure
Authority	Autonomy	Balance
Beauty	Boldness	Compassion
Challenge	Citizenship	Community
Competency	Contribution	Creativity
Curiosity	Determination	Fairness
Faith	Fame	Friendships
Fun	Growth	Happiness
Honesty	Humor	Influence
Inner Harmony	Justice	Kindness
Knowledge	Leadership	Learning
Love	Loyalty	Meaningful Work
Openness	Optimism	Peace
Pleasure	Poise	Popularity
Recognition	Religion	Reputation
Respect	Responsibility	Security
Self-Respect	Service	Spirituality
Stability	Success	Status
Trustworthiness	Wealth	Wisdom

Question 4: What are ways to generate income?

Then the next question I want you to answer is what are ways to generate income? Now, I'm not only talking about what you're currently doing or something that you think you can do. I'm asking you to do a brainstorm of all the different ways you can think of for a person to create income.

It could be having rental property. It could be writing a book or doing speaking engagements. It could be teaching or training by holding workshops and events. It could be working for someone else. It could be selling a specific product. Whatever it is, just go crazy here. Write out every single thing you can think of that can be done to generate income.

After you've written out your answers to these four questions, I want you to put on your imagination cap before answering the final question.

Take a moment and let go of all limitations and boundaries. You're going to dream with God.

Question 5: What skills, passions, values and income avenues can I combine?

Get very creative and look at the answers to the previous questions and find ways to connect them together. So, grab a skill, grab a passion, grab a value, and grab an income avenue then combine them together to create what I call Prongs of Purpose™.

As you are making combinations, don't judge them. Don't think about the viability of it or how realistic it is for you to be able to accomplish it. Allow yourself to be imaginative. Really, no idea is a bad idea in this phase. We'll weed them out later. Simply go through the process of brainstorming and making those combinations.

Once you've finally gotten to the point where you don't think you can make any more combinations between your answers go back and review each of the combinations. I promise you as you review them, you will start to see a reoccurring theme.

At the core of that theme is your purpose. Truth of the matter is, the majority of us actually know deep down what our purpose is. It has just gotten squashed down and buried because of people telling us what we can't do, life circumstances, and various different things.

This causes our purpose to become callused over where it takes a little excavation in order for you to actually uncover it again. I do want to give you this one caveat. If you are just starting the process of identifying what your purpose is, recognize it truly is a process. You may not get down to the exact thing in this, in this first exercise, but you will be well on your way. Commit to the process.

Commit to the process.

For example, when I first started tapping into my purpose, my overarching theme was to help women. I wasn't sure how, but as I started moving out and acting upon what I felt the calling was, gradually it became more and more clear. I realized, what I didn't really want to do and what I really enjoyed. I began fine tuning it as I went along the process.

This has been a multiyear process. It didn't happen for me overnight. Now if you can get right down to your core purpose, awesome! But if you don't uncover it right away, it's okay. Just commit to the process of continuing to search and digging deep within you to uncover what it is God has really called you to do.

Now you have a list of ways to make money drawn right out of your core purpose. Remember at the offset, I said your prosperity or your abundance is directly tied to your purpose. But here's the thing, your purpose isn't just for you.

Yes, your wealth, your abundance, your prosperity is tied to it, but it's not just for you. It is for other people as well. Your purpose is intended to serve others. If you don't actually do the work to tap into what your purpose is, then there are people who need you and what you bring to this world which will miss out on your special gift.

Once you've actually done the exercise and you have the various ways you can generate income, take a look at which one would be the easiest for you to get started on.

I call this the low hanging fruit. Look for your low hanging fruit. Look for the one thing that will be the easiest for you to get started on now.

Next create an action plan to get moving in the direction of it so you can start generating income. As you start working on it and perfecting it, then you can move into the next area that would be the easiest for you to shift into. As you move along the journey things will get clearer for you.

I hope this exercise has helped you get closer to your purpose and that you are committing to the process of fully uncovering it. I want you to be prosperous. I want you to have all the abundance and prosperity God has for you.

The way that you're going to do it is by shifting into what he created you to do. As you make the shift, you will run into some resistance. You'll discover your personal limits. In the next chapter, I'll share some strategies for stretching those limits so you can increase your capacity.

CHAPTER SEVEN

Increasing Your Capacity

Beloved, I wish above all things that thou mayest prosper and be in health, even as thy soul prospereth. ~ 3 John 1:2

The biggest problem we face when we want to achieve big goals or grow a successful business is a cap on our capacity. Now, what do I mean by that?

The scripture says in 3 John 1:2, I wish above all things that you would prosper and be in good health even as your soul prospers.

There's a reason why God wants us to grow or prosper in our soul. For clarification purposes, your soul is made up of your mind, your will and emotions. Because our soul is essentially the thermostat that determines the amount or the level of success we can experience. It could be financial success. It could be success emotionally or socially. No matter what, our soul is what regulates our success levels.

Most thermostats now days have an automatic setting. Meaning, you set the temperature and if it drops below the setting, the heat will kick on to bring your home back up to the set temperature. Same thing goes in the reverse. If your house gets too warm or goes above the thermostat is setting, the air conditioning will turn on to return the temperature back down to whatever the thermostat is set at.

Our soul acts in the same way. Our wealth, our success, our prosperity, all of that is determined by the capacity level of our soul. When we find ourselves plateaued in areas of our life it is because we are at our maximum capacity our soul is able to handle.

> *Our wealth, our success, our prosperity, all of that is determined by the capacity level of our soul.*

Just like the thermostat set to auto, if we go above or below our capacity, some kind of way we will end up back at that level with which we are comfortable with. In order to have sustained growth we must increase our capacity. By using the parable of the talents, I'm going to share six ways to do just that. But first, let's read through the parable.

This comes from the book of Matthew, chapter 25:14 - 30.

> [14] For the kingdom of heaven is as a man travelling into a far country, who called his own servants, and delivered unto them his goods.
> [15] And unto one he gave five talents, to another two, and to another one; to every man according to his several ability; and straightway took his journey.
> [16] Then he that had received the five talents went and traded with the same, and made them other five talents.
> [17] And likewise he that had received two, he also gained other two.
> [18] But he that had received one went and digged in the earth, and hid his lord's money.
> [19] After a long time the lord of those servants cometh, and reckoneth with them.

²⁰And so he that had received five talents came and brought other five talents, saying, Lord, thou deliveredst unto me five talents: behold, I have gained beside them five talents more.
²¹His lord said unto him, Well done, thou good and faithful servant: thou hast been faithful over a few things, I will make thee ruler over many things: enter thou into the joy of thy lord.
²²He also that had received two talents came and said, Lord, thou deliveredst unto me two talents: behold, I have gained two other talents beside them.
²³His lord said unto him, Well done, good and faithful servant; thou hast been faithful over a few things, I will make thee ruler over many things: enter thou into the joy of thy lord.
²⁴Then he which had received the one talent came and said, Lord, I knew thee that thou art an hard man, reaping where thou hast not sown, and gathering where thou hast not strawed:
²⁵And I was afraid, and went and hid thy talent in the earth: lo, there thou hast that is thine.

²⁶His lord answered and said unto him, Thou wicked and slothful servant, thou knewest that I reap where I sowed not, and gather where I have not strawed:

²⁷Thou oughtest therefore to have put my money to the exchangers, and then at my coming I should have received mine own with usury.

²⁸Take therefore the talent from him, and give it unto him which hath ten talents.

²⁹For unto every one that hath shall be given, and he shall have abundance: but from him that hath not shall be taken away even that which he hath.

³⁰And cast ye the unprofitable servant into outer darkness: there shall be weeping and gnashing of teeth.

#1 Be a good steward over what you have.

What we have monetarily is directly proportionate to the level we can handle or our capacity to steward. There were three servants and each was given a different amount of talents. The first servant and the second servant were good stewards over what the lord gave them and doubled the amount of talents they were originally given. But the third servant, who was only given one talent, hid the one he received. He was not a good steward over that which the lord had given him.

By doing business with or utilizing the gifts, talents, skills and abilities God has given you, you are being a good steward over those them. The scripture says the lord he "delivered unto them his goods."

The gifts, skills, talents, and abilities you have in you, are gifts given by God and he is expecting a return on his investment. When Jesus comes back, He wants to see what He's given you has increased. So being a good steward over what God has blessed you with is the very first tip for being able to increase your capacity.

#2 Be faithful in your service.

A lot of us tend to be all in one moment and then we back off the next. You can even see it in church attendance. One Sunday you're in service. The next Sunday, you might not be, or you might be there for two or three weeks in a row and then you're gone for a month. It is the same way with our finances or in our business, especially when you're starting a brand-new business.

You have to be consistent. You have to be faithful in serving, serving your customers, your clients, serving those on your job, serving those in your community. Whatever it is that God has given you to do, you need to be faithful in doing it.

#3 Don't be afraid to take risks.

Don't be like the third servant who took the talent and buried it for fear of losing it. That's really what it all boils down to. He said he knew the lord, his master, was a hard man who reaped where he did not sow. He was afraid if he tried to do business with the one talent he was given, he would lose it.

Too many people don't act on what they feel called to do because of fear. But by not taking risks, you never reap the reward. Life and business are all about taking risk. Putting yourself out there.

I can tell you right now, you won't always get it right. You will make mistakes. We all do. But I get it, putting yourself out there is uncomfortable. However, I encourage you to get comfortable with being uncomfortable because you will never find out if you can gain the reward if you don't take the risk.

#4 Do different to get different.

I like to say it this way. In order to have what you've never had, you have to be willing to do what you've never done. A lot of times we don't have more or our capacity is capped because we're continuing to do the same things over and over that have gotten us to the level of success or the level of financial prosperity where we are.

However, if we want to go beyond that, if we want to increase our capacity, if we want to have more finances more freedom, or whatever it is you desire more of, you have to be willing to do something different. If you want to meet more people or change your circle, you have to get out and go places you've not gone before.

If you want to reap more financial gains, then you're going to have to do something different so you can get more. Maybe you need to start a side job or seek a promotion. Perhaps you need to create a new product or service. Whatever it is, do something different so you can get different results.

#5 Use your gift.

Again, this goes back to stewardship. Don't bury what God has given you. Use it to serve others and I guarantee you there is a whole population of people who needs your gifts, skills, talents, and abilities because they're not necessarily good at it.

Often times we take for granted our gifts because they come so easy to us. But there are a great deal of people who it doesn't come easy for and they would be willing to either pay you to do it for them or to teach them how to do whatever it is.

For example, video editing. I started actually editing my own videos. Before I would just put them out there, mistakes and all. It's been a learning curve. I've had to watch a lot of YouTube videos and not be afraid to make mistakes. Now I have increased in that skill.

However, I wouldn't have been able to do it if there weren't someone who decided to share their gift and put up a video on YouTube on how to edit videos. Someone out there needs you. An entire group of people needs your gift. So, don't be afraid to use the gift that you have for monetary or financial gain.

For those of you who struggle to charge for your services, I have a scripture to help you out.

> *He that withholdeth corn, the people shall curse him: but blessing shall be upon the head of him that selleth it. ~ Proverbs 11:26*

#6 Walk by faith.

Everything we do, we have to do it by faith. We have to believe God is with us and that he has given us exactly what it is we need in order to be successful. Stepping out on faith can be a little bit scary, but that is the way we are called to live our lives.

The scripture says "the just shall live by his faith" (Habakkuk 2:4b) and "without faith it is impossible to please" God (Hebrews 11:6). I know as a believer, you want to be able to please God. Walking by faith is the way you do it.

Yeah, it's scary. Yes, you may not know if it's going to work out, but you will never find out if you don't ever take that first step to walk by faith.

Start today implementing these tips into your life so you can increase your capacity and experience more in your business and life.

Final Thoughts

If you've read this book from cover to cover, by now you should be fully persuaded God wants you to walk in abundance. The avenue He uses to bring abundance to us is our purpose. It is only when we fully align with His purpose for our lives we experience true prosperity and fulfillment.

My prayer is you will not just be inspired by the contents but provoked to action. Dreams and visions don't work unless you do. You are now armed with the information and strategies to take the first steps toward pursuing your purpose and manifesting prosperity.

It won't always be easy but it will always be worth it. Now get out there and...*Position Yourself to Prosper!*

Acknowledgments

This book never would have come to fruition if it weren't for some pretty amazing people supporting me along the journey.

First and foremost, I want to thank The Father for entrusting me with this message for His people. I pray it makes you proud.

To my loving and patient husband, Alex, who endured many takeout meals and days separated from me by a closed office door. Thank you for believing in me, proof reading my drafts, encouraging me to be patient and put out my best. I love you Babe!

Mom and Dad, thanks for always telling me I can do anything I put my mind to. Your love and support mean the world to me. To my mini me, Alexia, you inspire me more than you'll ever know. Thank you for cheering me on and always being present when you're needed the most. I love you, pumpkin!

I can't close without thanking a few women who held me accountable to the process. My business bestie, Dr. Laci Robbins, thanks for the prayers, support, and words of encouragement. Shannequa Cannon, it is because of you I took this message and put it to paper. You totally convinced me it would be easy. While it wasn't, it was definitely worth it. Finally, my sister spotters, Consuela Hill, Anika Wilson, Denise Smith, Verlonda Johnson, Nicole Everett, Barbara Williams, Dr. Judy Mandrell and so many others who it would be impossible to name – Thank you for spotting me!

About the Author

Trasetta Alexander is the Owner of Trasetta Alexander Enterprises and Host of the T.E.A with Trasetta Podcast. Her kingdom purpose is to empower the people of God to shift into their God-given purpose to create the life of abundance they desire.

As a faith-based business and productivity coach, Trasetta teaches her clients how to clarify, prioritize and monetize their purpose, through proven success strategies.

She shares empowers audiences with practical wisdom for pursuing purpose and inspires them by weaving in personal testimonies of her own triumphs and missteps. Event attendees always walk away prepared to take immediate results driven actions.

Trasetta is married to Pastor and Best-Selling Author, William Alexander and has an adult daughter,

Alexia. She holds a Bachelor's degree in social work from Thomas University and has over 25 years of experience in business operations management, across Fortune 500 companies, as well as, government and university systems.

She is a breast cancer survivor, mentor to girls and women, ordained minister and praise team leader. Trasetta believes no one is successful alone. Success comes through clarifying your vision, creating an action plan and developing a network of success partners.

Stay Connected:

Email: trasetta@trasettaalexander.com
Website: www.trasettaalexander.com
Facebook: @SpeakerTrasettaAlexander
Facebook Group: Kingdom Purpose Pursuers
Instagram: @TrasettaAlexander
Podcast: T.E.A. with Trasetta

To inquire about having Trasetta speak at your event, email trasetta@trasettaalexander.com.

Also by Trasetta Alexander

Available at trasettaalexander.com/books

www.ingramcontent.com/pod-product-compliance
Lightning Source LLC
Chambersburg PA
CBHW030944090426
42737CB00007B/534